Original Clichés

Also by Rob Walker

tropeland (Five Islands Press)
policies & procedures (Southern-Land Poets, Garron Publishing)
phobiaphobia (Picaro Press)
micromacro (Seaview Press)
sparrow in an airport (New Poets Ten, Friendly Street Poets/
Wakefield Press)
Thirty (Friendly Street Poets anthology/Wakefield Press
– as co-editor with Louise Nicholas)

Rob Walker

Original Clichés

For all the dedicated English teachers of
Cowandilla Primary (1958–65)
and Plympton High (1966–70).
No doubt they are all dead.
May they rest in peace during their
Eternal Long Service Leave.

Thanks to journalist Chris Pash, who triggered the idea for
this collection with his regular blog Cliché of the Week,
which ran from 2010 to 2013.

Original Clichés
ISBN 978 1 6041 127 5
Copyright © text Rob Walker 2016
Cover: *Grandma Lyn and Rainbow* by Amelia Walker

First published 2016 by
GINNINDERRA PRESS
PO Box 3461 Port Adelaide 5015 Australia
www.ginninderrapress.com.au

Contents

An accident waiting to happen	9
cliché anti-verse	11
A house of cards	12
After the climax	13
austerity measures	14
breaking bread / the mouse in the shed	15
pearl	16
cautiously optimistic	17
clinging to life	18
Love is blind	20
dying moments	21
The politician	22
evil root	23
iconic	25
ignored	26
A Better World	27
learning the language	28
less is more	29
ugly as sin	30
milk and honey	31
Daddy longlegs	32
on the other foot	33
Octophobia. The fat lady sings	34
geniophobia	35
Eisoptrophobia	36
poster child	38
reaching for the stars in the lower socio-economic suburbs	39
Mutton Jeff	40
shallow graves	41
floods from above	42

jazz channel	43
The *koan* before the *satori*	44
shrouded in secrecy	45
feral cat under a bridge	46
water under the bridge	47
Bath, England	48
in the steam train at Darjeeling station	49
moon anti-poem	50
phone conversation	51
lemonsong	52
sitting in the empty house	54
secret life of a bubble	55
sweeper	56
flood and desert	57
George the Younger	58
flow-on effect	59
On the road to Minnamurra	60
then one morning	61
Vietnamese dragons	62
The last resort	63
memory of Japanese moon viewing	64
Moon lantern festival, Adelaide	65
Symphony Under the Stars	66
before the poetry workshop at tatachilla lookout, Blyth	67
insomnia	68
Grrr…	69
Time of your life	70
unpacking	71
The owl speaks	72
two poems for my granddaughter	75
a rose	76
	77

absolute frontage	78
tethered	79
middle-aged Casanova	80
Love poem	81
rising	83
A cup	85
The Fresh People Food	86
Whitegoods Christmas	87
My left hand	88
A year of happiness	89
Ode to the Penis	90
worst-case scenario	91
kitchen conversation	92
this room	93
rock paper scissors	94
shall I compare thee?	95
Breaking mother's back	96
Bubbles of reality	97
speech of parts	99
Notes	100
Acknowledgements	103

'Let's have some new clichés.'

Samuel Goldwyn

'Only in art were there clichés; never in nature. There were no ordinary human beings. Everybody was born with surprise inside.'

Jincy Willett, *The Writing Class*

'The reason that clichés become clichés is that they are the hammers and screwdrivers in the toolbox of communication.'

Terry Pratchett, *Guards! Guards!*

'It is a cliché that most clichés are true, but then like most clichés, that cliché is untrue.'

Stephen Fry

Clichés can be quite fun. That's how they got to be clichés.'

Alan Bennett, *The History Boys*

An accident waiting to happen

purposeless and alienated, a coexisting *anomie* and *ennui*
a concatenation of the unrelated   I lurk on street corners
planning the intersection of vehicles.

delayed by traffic light whim or
leaving home moments earlier you leave   yourself
vulnerable to my coordinate points.

I am the hay bale awaiting synchronicity
of temperature   and humidity
to interrupt   a firefighter's dinner.

I am the thrown match which may peter out
or destroy the entire national park,
the oily rag in the shed.

I am the outdated nuclear reactor
behind the low seawall
waiting for the plates to move.

I am the occasional freight train,
the unsignalled crossing,
the sleepy motorist.

I am the barely submerged snag in the murky river,
                the sharemarket software trigger
programmed to sell   sell   sell.

I am the scissors in the hand of the running child
the gun in the glovebox,
gathering ions in cumulonimbus
above the golfer on the fairway,
the jet engine's invisible hairline fracture,
the tiny blood vessel in the brain under pressure

I am the one flake of snow
that begins the avalanche.

I am unstring theory.

I am tired of waiting,

so tired…

cliché anti-verse

in the cliché anti-universe

police are not baffled by the criminal
who had an unlucky escape

the opposition leader's raft of measures
sinks as all options fall off the table

the PM hits the ground walking
facing a downhill battle

vegans flesh out proposals.
meat is doing it tough.

in the third kitchen drawer down
a fork is balanced on a knife edge,

an accident not waiting to happen.

A house of cards

His name means Light. When he smiles the sun shines.
He is screaming because the door is usually open.
Today it is closed.

His autism blows storms from unexpected directions.
He attempts something new. Another child's comment.
A routine is changed.

The flimsy edifice of his confidence is raised, razed.
Even the worst tempest abates.
His screams subside.

Each day his teacher steadies his hand, helps
him to reconstruct the house of cards
named resilience.

After the climax

Please don't refer
to my bipolar mood swings.

You came here to have your fun with me.
I gave you fun.

You said I scared you, a nervous laugh
as you came along for the ride.

We've had our ups and downs
but we stayed together.

Even when you swore *never again*
you always came back for more and
never complained during the climax.

Climb on me one more time.
I KNOW I'm being hysterical!

What do you expect
from an emotional
roller coaster?

austerity measures

in the sixties we measured
milk by the pint and ships
by the galleon

we did the hard yards
inched our way to success
LSD was pounds shillings and pence

if a kid said he wanted a wii
you pointed to the toilet.

breaking bread / the mouse in the shed

Yorke Peninsula mouse plague, April 2014

we fed them poisoned wheat.
we fed them a multitude of products with cool names
like Talon, Tomcat, Bromakill and Ratsak
and still they kept coming.

Phil rigged up water traps, wine bottle pirate-planks with peanut
butter in welcoming throats over oceans of water in plastic buckets.
One trap drowned 93 in one night. The death toll mounted,
surpassed 250 in a single night.
Even Job would've lost his patience.

I came eyeball-to-eyeball with one fat little sucker in the boat shed.
He (it seemed like a he) was nibbling the fat which had dripped
from last night's barbecued T-bones
he paused ever-so-briefly before resuming his high-cholesterol repast,
sitting there a little obese in his brown mohair suit.
I wondered if mice became bored all wearing that same mousy hair.
were there blondes or individualists with blue or red
à la Sally Jenkinson?

I didn't kill it.
I can exterminate them in their hundreds
but not one
not one who's looked into your eyes
not one with whom you've shared a meal.

pearl

i am a pearl
and the oyster
is my world

cautiously optimistic

i truly believe
that the glass

is half-full.
of poison.

clinging to life

(for Lyn)

your mother worked her magic on every baby she could get
her hands on
engaged them with lilt of voice   sky blue eyes & smile
they'd stop mid-cry and laugh   she rocked / back-patted
incorrigible bawlers into blissful unconsciousness

you inherited this and more
you're a nurturer yes
but also plain bloody-minded.
dead be buggered!

you'd plunge wind-exposed apparent rigor-mortis-chilled lambs
into buckets of warm water and have them calling *maaahhh!*
drinking contentment in five minutes

you'd low-heat stillborn chickens in the frypan till they peeped Life
resuscitate ducklings and goslings overnight
in cardboard cartons by the combustion stove

reluctant ewes weren't permitted to reject lambs.
while i'd throw the sheep on its back
you'd force lamb's mouth to teat and hand-milk the mother
until both were resigned and surrendered to Life.

you'd smear vicks vaporub on orphans to dupe ewes into adoption
bottle feed poddy calves, pry open infected pink eyes
squeeze in golden ointment

inject chooks with penicillin.
no animal would dare
defy you with Death.

i know your secret of Life:

persistence.
        your mother's nurturing.
                your father's stubbornness.

Love is blind

wrinkles ironed out
your skin diffused a youthful
                                        glow

botox?   lipo?
cheeky implants?
                                        no

twenty years just melt away
dear   all I have to
                                        do

is leave
my glasses   by the
                                        radio

dying moments

the horizon a mathematical line dividing an almost-white
grey of air　　　　and a silver-mirrored plane of fluid

there is a small bird flying high over lake alexandrina
a black dot moving like an arrow　 dividing
the infinity of the future ahead
and the eternal past behind

the black gift a mere
moving pinpoint

        named
present.

by
the time
we recognise
its existence each
moment has become   the past.
                        every moment is dying.

The politician

Going forward we'd be backward if
>we didn't have a goal to look forward to.
>>Let me make this crystal clear. Crystal clear.

We'll take our whole raft of measures on board,
>unpack it and run with it. Everything is on
>>the table and I'm not ruling anything in or out.

I've said this before.
>Let's be consistent about this
>>going forward.

Down through the years I'll hit the ground
>running an uphill battle on the slippery slope
>>on the downward spiral.

>>We've been inundated and left
>hung out to dry
in the 24-hour spin cycle.

But it's crystal clear.
>Going forward we'll be,
>>er, going forward.

evil root

Or fall evil, too
I rot of all love

                    All vie for loot,
                    flail over loot
                    I'll rave of loot. I fall over loot

Frail love loot…
I'll love too far
All love of riot

                    For I to all love
                    All love of trio
                    Or all love of It…

I loft oral love
Till love of oral
Or flail to love

                    I love to floral.

Flora. Evil tool.
Veto floral oil
Flora. Vile loot.

                    All veil of root
                    of all live root
                    All of root, vile

All love, if root
All vie for tool
Flair love tool

                I'll rot a love of,
                Or a love of lilt.
                fill a love root

Overfill a tool
Overfool a lilt
to foil all over…

                Or fall evil too
                or loll, if ovate

I'll avert a fool
Or I, tall of love
Liar of lovelot

                Love. Trial. Fool.
                Vital fool role
                Air of lovetoll

For I allot love

                              Root of all evil.

iconic

in the radiology room waiting

holding our future in nervous hands
we come with X-rays – icons
in large envelopes with corporate logos

queue for the Delphic Oracle
who divines the auspices
like chook entrails.

this arcane analysis
reading the stars within.

ignored

i know they all think i'm overweight,
my skin has a few more wrinkles.

i long to overcome this social phobia
to overwhelm the shyness
just to chat and laugh with everyone
at this cocktail party

i'm a nobody, gauche and clumsy.
how is it possible that i remain unnoticed?

i'm taller than average
but my hide isn't impervious.
i'm sensitive. i remember the names of everyone here.

how can it be
that everyone here
ignores the elephant
in the room?

A Better World

Money is mute.
Humility talks.

Landmines are consumed by
dung beetles overnight.

People have the confidence of cats,
the loyalty of dogs.

Every word is a dollar to be spent wisely.

Every child is declared a National Treasure.

Children conduct workshops for parents
on Spontaneity and Optimism.

Conformity is tolerated.
Uniqueness celebrated.

learning the language

for my granddaughter at two each word is a revelation
the recognition that every sound represents
a real world thing   an idea in her head

ka means a change of scenery or visiting new faces.
at first she over-generalises & buses and trucks
share this *car* moniker too.

the sea is *big wet*. waves are *bubble*.
grandpa and banana are both *nana*.
she learns *no* before yes   knows *mama* and *dada*

she apes everything i say studying my lips and tongue intently.
can you say car?   *ka*.
holds her hand up like a toddler traffic cop & says *stop*!

can you say boat? *boat*. stop? STOP! she laughs eyes sparkling
like the sea at brighton. stop the boats? STOP THE BOATS!

she's precocious. already has the vocabulary
and the political maturity of the australian
electorate, cabinet and prime minister.

less is more

(woo confessions of a breatharian)

i found
i could live
on less.
the cream in the coffee
was first to go.
then the sugar.
then the coffee.
i ate less.
my soul grew.
my food was fresh air
and sunlight.
but the air was too dense.
i was putting on weight.
i cut back on the breathing.
nutrition from the sun
increasing the kilos,
i reduced
my exposure,
lived in a
darkened box.
no food.
no water
memory.
nirvana
coming
just
minutes
before
my
early
death

ugly as sin

Sri Darbar Sahib, The Golden Temple, Amritsar, India

he looks out from his *mamtee*
in a square island in sweet ambrosial nectar
at the clouds and blue reflected in
Holy waters.
the scaffolded jujube tree

a glorious cacophony
the museum of martyrs
a snaking line of devotees
a swaying mile of faces

drawn under the arch
below a rainbow
of turbans

expressing his love
and devotion
with a rag

polishing rails and orbs of gold
to see black nectar pools
in his own shining eyes

looking back
at smiling
marble teeth

and hands rubbing
out the filth
of sin

milk and honey

returning to
Adelaide from India
back to the land of plenty
in an arc you descend through
a mist banking over the Hills where
you live comfortably with your cows and beehives
descending the Marden foothills where your daughter studied last year
North Adelaide where you came close to going crazy (again) in 96
Thebarton's Western Teachers' College of the seventies.
Cowandilla where you went to primary school
Richmond   centre of childhood
touching down near the
place of your birth.
reliving your life
in four minutes
in reverse

Daddy longlegs

Pholcus phalangioides

a single grain of wheat
in a dot-to-dot
jointed-hair puzzle

seed body hanging,
hub of a web of legs
a father xmas thistle

spastic swastika sucking
redback juices.
a manic harpist

opposite spokes in
tandem   unspoken

inevitably inhabiting some
dark vertex of
a cube

on the other foot

It's a vessel for a foot,
        not a fitting gift for Cinderella.

A boot
is a welder's friend,
        not the best glass for champagne

A boot
is the natural enemy of the football,
        not welcome in Tea Ceremony

A boot
is callused from a life in the factory,
        not de rigueur for Swan Lake.

A boot
is growing weary of the smell of feet

A boot
is not a vegan

A boot is Canadian for *approximately*

A boot is not romantic
        A boot is not on the other foot.
              Nor does it want to be.

A boot is to a slipper as a giraffe
        is to an analogous relationship.

        Discuss.

Octophobia. The fat lady sings

2 is fine.
Even squared.
Cubed is out of the question.
Bingo! The quaking begins.
Even one fat lady is one too many.
She begins to sing
as infinity stands on its head.
∞

geniophobia

she wants a man whose jaw's in a permanent state
of recession…

her nightmare is all-night tv
celebrities prominent in all the wrong places.

grilled by Leno. old movies with Kirk Douglas,
his gash a ravine between bald hills.

the infomercial features Barry Mackenzie
and Chesty Bond.

she wakes in a sweat at 4 a.m.
halfway through a soap

where all the men poke their
unmentionables at her.

They are neither Bold
nor Beautiful.

Eisoptrophobia

self-reflection is dangerous.
that man pretends to be you
but he knows nothing,

except his left hand knows
what your right's doing.
his asymmetric face

the obverse of yours,
unknown
to your friends.

he watches you shaving.
flashes his teeth. ejects adolescent
pimples at you.

knows your every flaw.
stares at you long enough
to make you feel guilty.

says good morning, goodnight,
avoids you for most of the day.
pops up in unlikely places.

men's rooms.
sideways glances from shop windows.
his twisted Andrew Lloyd Webber face

glares back at you from the backs of spoons.
keeping tabs on you.
always mocking.

reminding you daily
of the passage of time.
you wish   you were a vampire
so you could be   rid of him.

poster child

    she
     is
   a moth
caught
 in a spot–
light ever
   spiralling
    upwards
      to fame
       acclaim
     increasing
     intensity
    warmth
   seduced
   to the
   dizzy
    heights
    of her
     own
      downfall

reaching for the stars in the lower socio-economic suburbs

we sing the clichés like a mantra. climb every mountain higher / follow your heart's desire / and when that rainbow's shining over you /

that's when your dreams will all come true.

it's the new secular catechism but when dad's in jail and mum's on drugs life's too overcast for rainbows / mountains are overwhelming and it's easier to just sit there and let the others climb in a life when options are limited you can only assert yourself by passive resistance. *let the others climb. you can't make me move. i'll just sit here like fat buddha. let the mountain come to mohammed. you can't make me do anything. let them reach for the stars. my life is mostly cloudy with a strong chance of rain and i can't even see your stupid stars.*

Mutton Jeff

over years unnoticed sounds fell
off the edge of his spectrum

compensating for the loss
of high-frequency sibilants and fricatives

by maxing out volume or turning up
treble on tvs & radios

hand-cupping an ear
to enlarge the receiving dish

later new digital hearing aids reminded him
of all he'd been missing

the biggest revelation in his garden,
his silent footfall in mulch now deafening

sometimes I go outside he confides
just to hear the crunch of the leaves…

shallow graves

these headline victims invariably
interred
just below the surface.

if only murderers would emulate
their back-page sporting heroes

and dig deeper.

floods from above

(landing in KL, 1/11/11)

flooded rivers haemorrhaging
silt into turquoise sea,
swirling, dispersing.

Macchiato poured into
a Blue Lagoon.

jazz channel

did lester young charlie parker dizzy gillespie and buddy rich at the
philharmonic in 1953 know that they would be the sound track to
turbulence and three layers of clouds of three different shades
of white travelling at three different speeds modal merging
with melodic to this diorama somewhere between
osaka and singapore as i down brandy
cointreau white wine and beer and
slip into a fog of an
indeterminate
decade
?

The *koan* before the *satori*

one hand is clapping in a forest,
                              unseen

the other crushed by a falling tree,
presumably
                also unseen

shrouded in secrecy

(Himeji, Japan)

all night snow drifted down down
like down from ducks

by sunrise it had built a quilt
to shroud the city.

covered the dirty grime
white on black.

snow infatuates, a flash
of white to blanket and disguise

but over time snow melts.

the dirt's still there.

feral cat under a bridge

it snowed last night and there you are.
i see you from the bus to himeji port.
a giant of cats.
a city's blanket of snow has not warmed you.

behind rusty grating inaccessible to humans
you catch early morning rays
warming your fur, licking your coat as
my adelaide hills cats before a fire

commuter cars and the bullet train rumble overhead,
background sounds to your daily struggle for life

commuters drag themselves to jobs
to put food on the table.
repetitive as construction hammers smashing
concrete   clanging steel.

you drag yourself into the sun
start sniffing out their disposals
for the first meal of your
sparkling fresh
new day

water under the bridge

every day i ride my bike past
the air-conditioning factory then stop
on *nobusue* beside the school

look down at the flowing senba river
the giant carp   monochrome goldfish
symbols of masculinity courage determination

watching them just below the clear surface
twisting muscular bodies swimming
upriver against the tide

feeling at one with them
so much like me
in continuous motion

facing upstream
getting nowhere

Bath, England

and did those feet
in ancient times

bathe here in
england's waters
green?

smells like it…

in the steam train at Darjeeling station

as we the privileged
sit in the warm carriage, they
stoke the boiler

and local children
in rags and snow
        risk lives
                arms
                        legs

to pick up fallen coals
to cool in puddles,
take home for cooking warmth.

and you wonder at their future
which could be
                education
                      employment

or the amputee beggar in the gutter
waving his stump like a
meal ticket.

moon anti-poem

the moon is not a muted lamp
the moon is not a balloon snagged in a tree
the moon is not a breast
the moon is not behind a veil
the moon is not mirrored
the moon is not a melon rind

the moon is just

the moon

phone conversation

our voices crack
                through wires

which hold us
                together,

tear us
                apart

lemonsong

in love's full bloom they made a gift
to us, a potted lemon tree.
we planted it.

as seasons turned in time it thrived
each flower held a tiny fruit
but their love soured

darling buds of May to June
withered under winter frost.
i hacked it back.

phoenix shoots spawned creamy blooms
and fruit as bright as painted suns
by five-year-olds

childhood green to lime to gold
with adolescent nipples
firm to soft

that rounded as they aged
then dropped

at base of trunk with compost scraps
then turned to white
to rejoin earth from whence they came

housewarming gifts
are oft-forgot.
this one endured beyond its pot.

its harvest was astringency
acerbic zest for stir fries
cakes and cordials

and window framed,
a thousand summer suns.

sitting in the empty house

we sit on the floor / backs to wall
in a not quite silence.

the acoustics
removed   along
with our possessions.

memories echoing back through years
bouncing off walls we'll never have to paint.

this shell of our lives where we
conceived and half-raised three children.

the baggage of thirty years   packed
blanketed and roped into a borrowed truck.

we look around at the hollowness.
we look around at each other.

then we turn backs to walls
walk out the front door
towards the future.

       extruded
    from loops, frothed
  up from baths & dishes
  i wobble my sphere
   forever exposing my
     surface, a fallen
       rainbow

secret life of a bubble

sweeper

london, 17 march 2003

between westminster abbey and the Houses he rakes the lawn of butts and litter

just down the road robin cook the leader in the House resigns brave but futile pissing in the wind

as a faint breeze blows from the thames depositing more leaves, papers

in the next few days the country will be at war but the sweeper will still sift litter

this detritus having no respect for Politics nor the Art of War

flood and desert

for Yahia Al-Samawy

The country you love is flooded with tyrants who abuse the name of Allah and *liberators* shouting *Justice* and *Freedom* whose faithless bullets and bombs   kill just the same.

you said
the tears
you shed

as you
wrote
the poem

would have
filled a cup
yet

you turn
these tears
to ink

spill it onto
the desert
of a page

and oases grow
where once
there was only

grit
to irritate
our eyes.

George the Younger

Said George
who chopped the cherry tree
I did it, Dad, for liberty

*I did it of my own volition
and with a willing coalition*

*a well-thought-out preemptive strike
to guard our oil and our Reich.*

His father beamed at him with joy,
winked and uttered
that's ma boy…

flow-on effect

Port Vincent

where once the she-oak grew on flats
        a coast has been *reclaimed*

        in this new age *marina*
        translates as *El Dorado*

high rollers washing in
flotsam of the affluent
        multiplier effect
yielded in its wake

        quandongs
are parasites
donating fruit.

Developers
say their fruit
will come in time.

On the road to Minnamurra

on the way to the national park
cabbage palms irrupt solo
from cropped
monoculture
paddocks

spectral
memories
of
intricate
rainforest

then one morning

carolling magpies become
        brake screeches

gargling frogs dissolve
to water in strangers'
        pipes

the roar of wind dissipates
to car exhaust
        rumble

and he realises
he has woken in
someone else's
        city.

Vietnamese dragons

I dream of dragons, smooth and scaled,
all kinds of dragons from Welsh myth to Puff.
And when I awake in the hotel room in Huế there is the dragon fruit
centimetres from my face in the bowl of tropical fruit,
a gift from hotel staff when we arrived yesterday.

today we walk the Purple Forbidden City,
see dragons painted on the roof, as statues, on walls, etched
on enormous ancient bronze urns and we spend the whole day
wandering the deserted site carrying the backpack with the fruit
in a plastic bag.

at lunchtime we climb the stone tower and sit cross-legged,
backs against a giant bronze bell and cut the dragon fruit into halves.
What a fantastic thing. A fruit designed by a committee,
the colours of a watermelon turned inside out,
centre like poppy-seed-flecked ice cream.

like that pink 70s Hare Krishna candle we kept at the shack
for power failures, intricate as an Indian temple in *jelabi* colours,
sliced and twirled, and every heatwave it softened & leaned
a little more one way,
a subcontinental Tower of Pisa.

we eat it to the rind
leaving pink stripes in the white
with our bottom front teeth,
looking down on the moat
in this land of dragons

The last resort

Hội An

the rooftop blue swimming pool is cracked and empty

rolling lawns taken by the rising tide

termites are encasing the outdoor furniture

the lipstick palms have baked in the sun

the ants have moved into the hotel's reception lounge

a relentless tropical yellow-green line of dots

removing the sugar from the bowl

memory of Japanese moon viewing

i miss the rabbit
in your upturned fullness,
clouds swirling in
miso soup

Moon lantern festival, Adelaide

children parade home-made lanterns,
glow-worming their way along
the banks of the Torrens.

a helium balloon lets go of its child
returns skyward like *Kaguyahime*.
i blink and it becomes a full moon.

Symphony Under the Stars

Thomas Rann plays Bruch's *Kol Nidrei* on a 309-year-old cello, Elder Park, 4 February 2006

A pair of pelicans beat wings in unison along the river's curve.
Clouds break as the sun seawards. The dome of the sky plays
through its changes   yellow/orange/gold.

Eucalypts silhouetted. The Convention Centre's curved tectonic
continued in the orchestra's sound shell. Darkening.
Brake lights from cars gliding across

the bridge wink approval. Streetlights scribble their light
on the River Torrens' black canvas. A musty smell
of barely moving water

air cooling & moistening with the setting sun. The lone cello's
woodiness speaks of warmth and sadness, its reedy voice

vibrating over fresh-mown lawns
washing over a becalmed audience

sound waves bypassing cerebrum
seeking a visceral

truth.

before the poetry workshop at tatachilla

i take a dirt road shortcut
communication road

another roadside memorial
damo was da man
scorched pine needles and bark
black earth
a heart of flowers threaded on a coat hanger
in our harts 4 eva
the decapitated steering wheel
leans against a she-oak
in a bed of
windscreen
crystals.
an upswelling of grief
bunches of decomposing flowers
fresh ones less than a day old
just another wasted young life.

damo was da man

lookout, Blyth

a faded wheaten shawl
drapes the land
worn through to red elbows,
folds and creases

the old lady
casually indifferent
in her stubble quilt
tired, sucked of life

waiting the rain

insomnia

a lone plover keens   flies
                    into a wall

                            of black

        a goods train near Blackwood
                  shudders in the cold

        a mopoke mourns the loss
of something

        a jittery dog yaps

                at its echo.

      all the rest

              is silent roar

Grrr...

months later when a nervous dog tells me
to back off, a denouement.

that boy had been trying to tell me the same thing
when I'd asked him to join the lesson.

those kids were laughing at him
and this was my first warning

if he were cornered
he would become violent.

rejected by both natural parents
a string of foster parents and GOM carers

his amygdala knew about self-preservation.
his body a 12-year-old boy
his brain a cornered animal, back to the wall.

niceties stripped down it's
You or Them.

his breathing takes over, sucking,
blowing through teeth and nostrils.

the rage begins.
the animal returns.

Time of your life

according to some teachers these boys are

Disengaged
        Apathetic
                Rebellious
                        Disruptive

yet at their last school assembly they play *wild thing* and
                              smoke on the water

as we all did
thirty years ago

then *time of your life*

now they're overnight successes   legends in their own
lunchtime

they laugh   unsurly eyes shining
invite me to join them
on bass
for *good riddance*

and afterwards ask
if I need help
to pack away
        the PA

unpacking

'A journey of a thousand miles begins with a single step.' Lao-tzu (604–531 BCE)

I'm attending this Advanced Skills Teacher conference
on the last reluctant day of my holidays.
Apparently the participants are at the beginning of a *Journey*.
The speakers tell us of *their* AST *journey*.

First we weigh ourselves down with jargon.
We have to take things *on board*.
It seems in contemporary times
we *unpack before* our odyssey.
We unpack our jargon,
jettison our emotional baggage.

As day wears on the itinerary becomes more tedious.
I reflect that I've had advanced skills for years –
good role model to thousands of students,
helpful mentor and colleague.

Like a well trained pussy cat I've leapt
through those flaming hoops.
Now it seems I have to do it all again,
perform my tricks consistently
for my Lion Manager,
get affidavits and documentation to state
that I have indeed jumped
through multiple rings of fire
over many years
then do it again
before a three-ring assessment panel.

I wonder what part of my teaching
and my life
I'll sacrifice to find the time.

Then the scales fall from my eyes
on this Damascan road.
In a blinding flash it is revealed
that my AST journey has ended
in a cul-de-sac
in a single
step.

A peckish bird has briefly knocked out part of the world's biggest atom smasher by causing a chain reaction with a piece of bread.

Bits of a French loaf dropped on an external electrical power supply caused a short circuit last week, triggering failsafe devices that shut down part of the cooling system of the giant experiment to probe the secrets of the universe.

The European Organisation for Nuclear Research (CERN) says the system was restored several hours after the incident last week while the multi-billion-dollar Large Hadron Collider was barely affected.

'The bird escaped unharmed but lost its bread,' CERN said in a statement.   The bird was believed to be an owl.

© AFP

The owl speaks

there are some things faster than light.
i know.
thoughts of a scampering mouse,

the twitch and glide of my feathers
which move even before i think.
the anticipation of talons.

the secrets of the universe reside in my head
not your giant machine smashing crumbs
yet tinier.

there are more things in the universe
than dreamed in your philosophy.
i am nature red in beak and claw.

i am quick to see,
quick to listen,
slow to speak.

harbinger of your demise
after the briefest of lives.
envy my omniscience.

your knowledge
is at its beginning.

two poems for my granddaughter

1 Amelia's foot

you arrive on life's ground floor ahead of time, low weight,
a prostrate marathon runner   my tentative finger
probes the humidicrib's mouth, strokes
your sole wrinkled from 37 weeks in your steaming amniotic
bath   toes splay back in pleasure, a gardenia softness
or is it a camellia, amelia?

such a tiny footprint on this carbon copy of my son
and his wife   a foot which has still to walk on
the earth.   where will these feet take you?

may they be places of self-confidence
       and joy beyond the pedestrian,
              beyond my imagination

2 Amelia on the beach at two and a half

she is maker and destroyer. shiva and vishnu in one cute package
can't decide whether she prefers building sandcastles or
smashing them down and after twenty repetitions
the castle becomes a head with seaweed hair
and cockleshell eyes until this is no longer
a challenge so she runs into the wind
flaps her arms at her sides
becomes a seagull
and flies away.

a rose

by any
other
name

wouldn't
be a
rose
really.

absolute frontage

on the tokyo river cruise in light rain
the commentator proud
of his river
his city its
bridges
points
out philip stark's
golden slug on the asahi
building but ignores the homeless
wrapped in blue tarps on the opposite bank
discarded as broken
umbrellas

tethered

Lands End, Cornwall

a knot of photo-taking tourists then   separated
a lone man in a blue parka against the lead-grey sky
holding an orange reel   flying a kite   tethered
to his exultant arm

mainland reaching further out over maen cliff
the sea diving and soaring with the falling cadences of gulls
an arc of arm and arc of string weightless as a pencil line

stacked granite slabs squatting on cliffs   thoughts of d-day
francis drake, chichester, pilgrim fathers cutting the string
what were their thoughts leaving plymouth
and passing this no return point?

chasing a new world.
soldiers who might return.
or not.

the kite restrained to motherland by an impossibly-thin umbilicus,
trying to leave, plunging dipping straining its radius.
there is no land's end.
it's 1 mile to longships and 28 to the scillies
and 3,174 to new york.

we are all of us anchored
                      to some piece of land,
                                      somewhere.

middle-aged Casanova

(after Carlos Williams)

so much depends
on a red
sports
car

a toupé

an

u
p
w
a
r
d
l
y

mobile
personal
assistant

&

    a
   r
  g
  a
 i
v

Love poem

(after Billy Collins)

You are the light that strikes horizontally in the final
        hour before sunset, the sun which paints gold
        everything it touches.

You are a struck match, welcome light in an emergency
        which gutters out in a night wind or burns my
        fingers. You are the odour
        of autumn apples in cartons in the laundry.

You are my rudder except when you are my anchor. You are
        my milestone and my millstone. You are both the
        pop and sigh
        of a champagne cork.

You are not the after-party empty beer bottles. You are
        certainly the twittering of blue wrens at a frequency
        I may not hear if I don't wear earplugs to band
        rehearsals.

You are definitely not the mournful cry of that damn mopoke
        on a summer's night or the blood-curdling shriek of
        a curlew like the wandering lost souls of the dead.

You are decidedly the tartness of that cherry pulp they put in
        the buns from the South Plympton Bakery. You are
        assuredly not the smell of dog turd in the tread of
        my sneaker.

You are probably the feel of a baby's breath on my cheek. You are arguably not the thin slice of a new moon discarded like a chewed finger nail.

You are everything in my universe. I hope I didn't go too far earlier with the millstone comment.

rising

after *High tide, Wynnum*, by Carole King, winner of 2014 Waterhouse Art Prize, South Australian Museum

1

i will rise up and offer
                        a reflection so much richer
                                        than any mirror
                        a trope of movement
and blurring of detail

2

                                        like the barmah choke
      or that girl who paddled you

              in her canoe on the edge of lake Tonlé Sap

                    and her permanent boat people

          who belong
to neither Cambodia   nor Vietnam

perched in pole houses   above the water's flow

          floating through a forest

inverted trees shimmering   swirling wobbling their

              hallucinatory solidity

when we watched little kids

        wading through water lapping

              under chins, schoolbooks on dry heads

3

    grey herons aka blue cranes with skewer beaks and 50s
slicked-back hair
on bleached river red gum fingers
royal spoonbills holding up their blunt cutlery just to
contrast
with a sky as azure as the kingfisher's underwing
a cormorant freeze-frames on a rock offering his shiny drying
back
rampant as a nazi icon.

    twice I have boated through flooded forests.

4

Here the Murray narrows
between Lakes Moira and Barmah

we cut the motor and drift in this perched river
centimetres higher than water on both sides of
clay banks grown stalagmite-like over time.
you expect a river in a valley, landscape
rising on either side yet here the view's
uninterrupted both ways with water
views below natural levees
lifting the flow
suspended
floating
above
land

A cup

                      is always weakest at the handle
        A cup is not a bouncing ball
A cup is a physically handicapped teapot

A cup is not the best seat in the house
        A cup is half a bra
A cup is not an anorexic toilet bowl

A cup is an upwardly mobile mug
        A cup is not prepared to take the rap
                      about that slip
            twixt it
        and the lip

A cup is the runt of the Crockery family
        A cup is not considering elopement with the dish
(or the spoon)

A cup is far from happy when it runneth over
        A cup is not enough for the caffeine addict.

        A cup is a glass   unclear
            of its purpose

The Fresh People Food

stuck in a 1980s time warp
the muzac bland, Mainstream
middle-of-the-road. nothing changes.
there is no War on Terror,   no poverty

just row after row after row of groceries
stacked in columns and battalions
soldiers erect and in uniform
And when the front line is consumed
the back is moved to the front.

nightfall. depletion. replacement.
night-fill boys are expendable too.
no award rates here.
individual items
non-essential.

the machine grinds on.

an illusion of changelessness.
continuous consumption.

broken packages put out of sight.
spills are wiped up
collateral damage.
profits are up.

clean.   tidy.
and nothing

appears to

change.

Whitegoods Christmas

        These dreams are stacked in aisles, white or stainless
As promises of Love and Labour lost.
        The pleasure's in the giving and it's painless
As credit cards and time defer the cost.

My left hand

sits on the page
resting its finger tips
silently crouching
watching

watching what
the right hand writes

writes rarely, clumsily
itself

itself subservient
to the dominant
right

always sinister
never dextrous

a lifetime as the
less-gifted brother
resentful

insecure less-feted
self esteem deflated

silent
it squats
there

plotting its
revenge

A year of happiness

that year the colours were more vivid and
intense. every moment lived felt like a minute.

every day was a month.
the year an entire lifetime lived.

sounds, temple-bell clear, still ring in
their ears. floating in an alternate world.

they wanted to taste every moment,
suck the juice from each experience.

it was the best year in a
lifetime of years,

a year too perfect
to be repeated.

Ode to the Penis

Shall I compare thee to a rubber band?
Thou art more flexible of bendage:
The toy that each boy has at hand;
Small wonder 'tis his favourite appendage:
Available in any shade desir'd,
Withstanding wear and tear or being abus'd;

With batteries not normally requir'd,
Improv'd performance each time it is used.
While other toys the little boy outgrowes,
His obsession like that other strange enigma
Tumescent thinge of wood (Pinocchio's)
Whose fantasies resulted in such stigma.

Diminishing returns will seldom figure;
The more 'tis play'd, the more it getteth bygger.

worst-case scenario

FADE IN: EXT. STEVE'S HOUSE – NIGHT

Tall, wide McMansion on a roomy plot of land.

Music pumps out. All the lights are on. Sound of laughter.

Hand-held camera enters the front door.

INT. STEVE'S HOUSE – CONTINUOUS ACTION

Clusters of REVELLERS dance and laugh in small knots. Everyone has a drink in their hand.

CUTE TEEN: Cool party, Steve!

STEVE (Good-looking, popular) smiles and nods…

CUT TO SCREEN IN PASSENGER JET COCKPIT

FX: The roar of engine –

SLOW FADE UP:

CO-PILOT: We have a warning light on the rear port!

PILOT: (deadpan) Starboard's just dropped out too.

AIR TRAFFIC CONTROL (V.O.): QA46? Do you read?

We hear SCREAMING ENGINES.

SMASH CUT TO: Aircraft plummeting onto Steve's house.

ROLL CLOSING CREDITS.

kitchen conversation

the cannabis in the saucer is
reflected in Russell Hobbs.

Russell sighs and lets out
a small puff of steam.

'It's not fair,' he wheezes.
'You make people laugh.

All I do is make tea and coffee.
I'm just the nigger of the kitchen…'

You can't say that! explodes marijuana
in a fit of psychosis.

Say African American!
'It's OK to call yourself nigger,' explains Russell.

'It's just offensive and non-PC
to use it on someone else.'

And so it was that the pot
called the kettle black.

this room

we are here together
in this room called poem

(i'll keep the conversation brief, reader,
because it is after all not an essay)

and by the end of the page
which is coming oh-too-soon

you will know a little of me
perhaps your lips may curl
ever-so-slightly into a wry smile

but i will know nothing of you
which is a pity because

i like to think that we
have so much
in common.

rock   paper   scissors

rock.

paper.

scissors.

in real life the rules flex.

necessity is invention's supporting mother
creativity (the father) having moved on…

bamboo erupts breaking bitumen
        paperbarks cleave rock in gorges
                time drips   water carves canyons

water eats rock

hollow cave's obverse
        is solid stalactites
                (rock born of water)

steel
        excavates
                rock

which melts
        to forge steel
                for scissors

ideas scratched on paper
        defeat scissors or swords
                ideas which

                                may even endure beyond rock

shall I compare thee?

and he's like
Hot AS

and I'm like
oh-my-god sort of thing

y'know?

and I'm like,
fully yeah, whatever

and he's like
OK…

and i'm just…
sort of   yeah…

it was so cool…

and i was

so not

Breaking mother's back

traditionally we avoided these pave   ment
faultlines. in a new age of no-fault   compensation
grade 4 boys take premeditated   aim
filling whole spinal units wit   h their own mothers.
maternity and traction go h   and-in-hand
a pandemic of chiropracti   c matricide.

Bubbles of reality

So here I am, a front-row seat
in Amsterdam, a cool-jazz beat
Modern Jazz Quartet they're called
It's '57. Urbane. Sweet.

Chamber music's Modern Age,
John Lewis piano-playing sage.
Lost in music's interplay
my seat jerks roughly towards the stage.

My earplugs and my iPod fall
I realise I'm not there at all
but on a bus with windows fogged
and in Japan I now recall.

It's hot in here but not outside
Commuters sleep all through the ride
We pass Himeji Castle, snow,
My reverie's abruptly died.

I wonder if I'm really here
an alien resident for a year
or back at home still sound asleep
alarm about to ring out clear…

And so it goes, banality,
the bubbles of reality
like Russian dolls each bubble pops
I doubt my person-ality.

And when I die will I be less
than all a bubble can compress?
And will the final burst reveal
a mere sphere   of nothingness?

speech of parts

I don't know what I metaphor.
I tried ten puns to make her laugh.
                No pun in ten did.

I'm a poet! I ejaculated   prematurely –
She just left me   dangling

a participle, part-disciple, part-adieu, *pas de deux*,
cut me to the Quink with her secateurs
               (non sequitur)

my heart cut up as a found poem
split   as an infinitive

I   am in the present,   tense.
She,   the past,   perfect.

Notes

'An accident waiting to happen': probably the first one I wrote where I mused on a cliché and created a poem by turning it inside-out.

'After the climax': I grew so tired of the 'emotional roller coaster' expression I just had to write about the ride from the roller coaster's point of view.

'The politician': if they're good for nothing else, our leaders are an excellent source of cliché and inspiration for absurdity.

'evil root': I went through a stage of attempting poems in anagram.

'learning the language': despite the cynicism of the poem, watching Amelia acquiring language has made me look at the whole process anew and to wonder at how rapidly young kids learn.

'ugly as sin': a visit to the holiest of Sikh temples allowed me to focus on a young boy whose faith, joy and devotion were expressed in the simple act of polishing.

'Octophobia': fear of the number 8.

'geniophobia': fear of chins.

'Eisoptrophobia': fear of mirrors and reflections.

'poster child': this could be about Britney Spears, Amy Winehouse or anyone else who sadly is overwhelmed by celebrity lifestyle.

'The *koan* before the *satori*': a *koan* is a paradox or riddle to be meditated upon (and often used in the training of Zen Buddhist monks.) A *satori* is a sudden enlightenment or spiritual awakening.

'secret life of a bubble': you could say that interpolating the title and the poem was putting the cart before the horse. But that would be a cliché.

'Flood and desert': my friend Yahia al-Samawy is a highly respected Iraqi poet. Imprisoned and tortured under Saddam Hussein's regime, Yahia fled and spent years in exile in Saudi Arabia before seeking asylum with his family in Australia. I met him through teaching his (now grown) children and our shared interest in poetry. Yahia is still widely remembered and regarded throughout the Middle East for his poetic imagery and opposition to both the privileged excesses of the Shahs and the brutal dictatorship of Saddam Hussein. His poetry in Arabic has won him the prestigious Prize of the Arab Union for Poetic Creativity. He continues to travel back – sometimes in dangerous circumstances – for guest appearances at writers' festivals. He has published more than twenty volumes of poetry in Arabic and one in English.

'moon lantern festival': Kaguyahime (princess Kaguya) comes from Japan's oldest (10th century) extant folk tale, often translated as 'The Tale of the Bamboo Cutter'. The mysterious girl is discovered inside the glowing base of a bamboo. She is adopted by the childless bamboo-cutter and his wife but must eventually return to her real home on the moon.

'Symphony Under the Stars': an annual free family concert featuring the Adelaide Symphony Orchestra and held on the lawned banks of the River Torrens.

'lookout, Blyth': written at the end of a very long drought near Blyth in South Australia's mid-north.

'Grrr…': GOM = Guardianship of the Minister, formerly 'ward of the state'.

'The Fresh People Food': in April 2015 Woolworths, one part of Australia's huge supermarket duopoly, was widely criticised for using its Fresh Food logo and font as 'Fresh in our memories' superimposed on the photos of Anzacs who died in the Gallipoli campaign. The advertising campaign was quickly abandoned.

'A year of happiness': this was about my wife Lyn and me after our life-changing 2008 living and teaching in Japan. Ironically, the opportunity repeated in 2012 for a second year 'too perfect to be repeated'.

'Ode to the Penis': no doubt many humorous poems have been written in history about this ridiculous appendage but probably not many as a variation of a Petrarchan sonnet. This version is two sestets with a rhyming couplet ending. Very classy.

'Worse-case scenario': obviously this relies on the original Italian-derived meaning of scenario – a written outline of a film or stage production.

'shall I compare thee?': this is a summary of a loud conversation between two teenage girls which I was forced to endure on the train from Blackwood to Adelaide. I was somehow reminded of the romantic work of Shakespeare or Keats.

'Bubbles of reality': written in the Persian *ruba'i* form.

'speech of parts': why not end a book of clichés with some really bad puns? No one was happier or more surprised than me when Les Murray selected this for *Best Australian Poems* back in 2005!

Acknowledgements

Some of the poems in this collection have been published previously. Thanks to the following journals, websites and anthologies.

Red River Review, November 2012, for 'an accident waiting to happen' and 'cliché anti-verse'.

Mindfields, edited by Ken Vincent & Jude Aquilina, Ginninderra Press, for 'A house of cards' originally titled 'The autistic boy'; these three poems also appeared in *tropeland*.

'an accident waiting to happen' was anthologised in *The Stars like Sand: Australian speculative poetry*, edited by Tim Jones, P.S. Cottier & Dr David P. Reiter, 2014, Interactive Publications, Carindale, Queensland, and *The infinite dirt: Friendly Street Poets 38* (edited by Jelena Dinic, gareth roi jones & Thom Sullivan).

ccmixter, Speck and others, who remixed parts of 'dying moments' as a musical piece 'a mere moving pinpoint', http://ccmixter.org/files/speck/41626.

Sandra Thibodeaux's poet-in-residence blog for 'A better world'; It later appeared in *Sorcerers and Soothsayers* Friendly Street poetry reader #35, edited by John Pfitzner & Tracey Korsten, Friendly Street Poets/ Wakefield Press, 2011.

Earlier versions of 'The politician', 'breaking bread', 'learning the language' and 'Grrr…' appeared on my own website www.robwalkerpoet.com during the daily NaPoWriMo poetry challenge April 2014.

Earlier versions of 'Evil root' and 'The fat lady sing's were in *phobiaphobia*.

'Mutton Jeff' and 'Time of Your Life' appeared in *Policies and Procedures*.

'Iconic' is the original version of what later became a collaboration with Maggie Ball in *Policies and Procedures*.

'The koan before the satori' appeared in *Mascara Literary Review* in 2008.

'moon antipoem' is the text of the 2007 Newcastle Poetry Prize (New Media) interactive poem, which was a collaboration with my son Matt; in the interactive version, the viewer clicks on a phase of the moon and constructs the poem in a random order.

Australian Poetry Journal 5.1 for 'Eisoptrophobia'.

New Poetry Down Under / Numbat for an earlier version of 'ugly as sin' (published as 'love as service'), 'George the Younger' and 'on the other foot' (as 'A boot').

Poetas del Mundo (Poets of the World) for 'Flood and desert'.

fourW twenty six New Writing (edited by David Gilbey), Wagga Wagga, NSW, 2015, for 'In the steam train at Darjeeling station'.

ABC Pool website (discontinued) for 'lemonsong'.

LiNQ, vol. 33, for 'Flow-on effect'.

Poetry Magazine (US), Vol. XIV, No. 2, Summer 2013, for 'Vietnamese Dragons'.

foam:e (March 2015) for 'memory of Japanese moonviewing'.

Illya's Honey (US), Vol .18, No. 2, for 'A cup and My left hand'.

Blue Giraffe 6 for 'shall I compare thee?'

Justin Lowe's bluepepper website for 'jazz channel' and 'The Fresh People Food'.

Friendly Street Poets website, 2008, for 'Whitegoods Christmas'.

Blast Magazine #3 and *phobiaphobia* for 'breaking mother's back'.

'Rock paper scissors' appears in *micromacro*; there are a number of remixed musical versions of it on ccmixter.org.

'middle-aged Casanova' is inspired by William Carlos Williams's 'Red Wheelbarrow'.

'Love poem' is inspired by Billy Collins's 'Litany'.

'Reaching for the stars in the lower socio-economic suburbs' quotes part of 'Reach' by Cathy Dennis and Andrew Todd, recorded by S Club 7, © 2000.

Best Australian Poems 2005, edited by Les Murray, and *Blur*, Friendly Street Poetry Reader #29, edited by Amelia Walker & Shen, 2005, for 'speech of parts'.

www.ingramcontent.com/pod-product-compliance
Lightning Source LLC
Chambersburg PA
CBHW070936080526
44589CB00013B/1534